Original title:
Shadows of Shade

Copyright © 2025 Creative Arts Management OÜ
All rights reserved.

Author: Dexter Sullivan
ISBN HARDBACK: 978-1-80566-672-1
ISBN PAPERBACK: 978-1-80566-957-9

Where Dreams Take Refuge

In corners dark where giggles gleam,
A rubber chicken sings a dream.
A cat in boots, oh what a sight,
Dances with glee, avoiding the light.

A hidden world where socks reside,
With mismatched pairs, they take a ride.
A pickle jar holds secrets tight,
While jelly beans plan a midnight flight.

Lawn gnomes whisper, trade their tales,
As paper boats plot wind-bound sails.
Tickling the breeze with goofy grins,
It's quite the place for silly wins.

So close your eyes and take a leap,
Where laughter's loud and dreams don't sleep.
Come join the fun, it's quite a spree,
In this wild realm, just you and me.

Textures of the Unseen

In the attic, dust bunnies play,
Racing along to a bluesy sway.
Chairs giggle when no one's around,
While the ceiling fan spins tales profound.

A pickle upside down declares,
That socks and spoons have dreams to share.
The wallpaper peels, hiding its art,
A masterpiece of the bizarre heart.

A toast to the mugs with mismatched eyes,
Who gaze at their fate with surprise.
They clink with cheers, in silly delight,
Toasting to nonsense under moonlight.

So weave your way through cluttered dreams,
In this odd little place, nothing's as it seems.
Join the fun, let laughter ring,
In a world where the unseen can sing.

Threads of Enigma

In a café, a cat wore a hat,
He sipped tea like a fancy brat.
But when he sneezed, oh what a sight,
The hat flew off, much to his fright.

A dog in the corner chuckled loud,
Said, "That cat thinks he's quite the crowd!"
But who invited the clumsy mouse?
He danced on the table – quiet as a house.

Faint Glimmers of Yesterday

A squirrel tried to juggle nuts,
But dropped them all – oh, how it struts!
With one on his head and two on his toes,
He thinks he's cool, but nobody knows.

An owl watched from a crooked branch,
Said, "Get it together, give it a chance!"
Yet as he spoke, he lost his grip,
And did a flip off the branch – a funny trip!

Veils of Dusk

The moon wore a veil, oh so rare,
A raccoon said, "It's a costume affair!"
But when the stars laughed and twinkled bright,
The moon blushed pink, what a silly sight!

A fox tried to dance, but tripped on his tail,
While fireflies giggled, chasing their trail.
They shone like diamonds, oh what a show,
As the fox spun around, almost fell in a row.

Whispers Beneath the Canopy

Under the trees, a frog lost his tune,
He croaked out a song, thought he was a boon.
But the crickets laughed, jumped into the act,
Harmony formed in a comical pact.

The raccoon joins in, with a beat on a log,
A wild jamboree, where none can procrastinate!
The owl hoots soft, trying to keep pace,
But with all the fun, he forgot his place!

Secrets Whispered by the Breeze

The gossiping wind, it does tickle,
With tales of the squirrel, quite a pickle.
A dance with the leaves, oh such delight,
As crickets join in, making the night.

A tree's best friend, it spills all the tea,
About raccoons plotting to steal your brie.
Mice in tuxedos, they waltz with grace,
While the owls keep watch, a wise little face.

Eclipsed by the Evening Sun

When the sun plays peek-a-boo with the ground,
The rabbits wear glasses; how silly they sound.
In their little bow ties, they hop with flair,
While the badger pretends he's the local mayor.

A comet of cheese streaks across the sky,
While birds dress in feathers of pie, oh my!
The shadows grow long, like jokes that don't land,
But giggles are the best; come join our band.

Beneath Layers of Illusion

Under the surface, a funny sight,
A turtle in sneakers, running with might.
He's racing a snail, who's sipping on tea,
While a frog plays the drums, as happy as can be.

The shadows play tricks, they pull pranks galore,
As owls wear sunglasses, while others adore.
A parade of the odd, a wild, wacky show,
Join the laughter parade; just take it slow.

The Graying of Day

As the sun says goodnight with a wink and a sigh,
The raccoon puts on a top hat, oh my!
With birds in tuxedos, they dance on a vine,
Creating a scene that's simply divine.

The stars come out with a giggle and roar,
As crickets join in, oh, what a chore!
But laughter lingers as night takes its hold,
And the moon makes a joke that's age-old and bold.

Glistening in the Half-Light

In the corner, a cat does slouch,
Chasing nothing, it's quite the pouch.
With a flick of an ear, it's gone!
Was it a ghost, or just a dawn?

Under the couch, a sock does hide,
Not a monster, just my pride.
With every creak, my heart does race,
Just the pizza delivery's face.

The Enclosed Stillness

In the closet, a sweater sighs,
Out of season, it waves goodbyes.
The old shoes whisper tales of fun,
Scuffed adventures, one by one.

Behind the door, a dust bunny hops,
Wearing my old sock, it never stops.
In the quiet, giggles burst,
Who knew that fur could quench a thirst?

Echoes from the Abyss

The bathroom mirror plays a prank,
With toothpaste swirls, my thoughts are blank.
A face within, it starts to grin,
Did I put on a mask or sin?

The toilet bowl forms a royal ring,
Where frogs practice their happy spring.
In every plop, a symphony swells,
The echoes dance like tiny bells.

Invisible Threads of Reality

My socks conspire to go astray,
One's in the wash, the other plays.
Caught in a spin, they tease and twirl,
A sneaky duo in laundry swirl.

Under the bed, a rumor starts,
That pizza crusts have stolen hearts.
They dance at night, in moonlight's grip,
When I'm asleep, they take a trip.

Where Daylight Meets Its End

When the sun lags behind the trees,
Night creatures stir with giggles and wheeze.
Bats in tiny capes fly around,
Chasing cats who leap with a bound.

A squirrel in tuxedo scurries with glee,
Holding a party for all to see.
The moon winks, a cheeky old friend,
While mischief brews as daylight bends.

Twilight's Ethereal Touch

The rabbits wear glasses and act quite grand,
Debating the grass—where's the best brand?
Fireflies giggle, making small trends,
As the night in its navy quietly blends.

A fox in a bowtie plays hopscotch with style,
While owls flip pancakes over in a pile.
The stars play tag, shining more vibrant,
As night slips in with a wink and a giggle so vibrant.

Cloaked in Mist

In the hush of the fog, a dance can be seen,
Goblins in pajamas launch javelins of green.
Whispers of laughter drift through the thrum,
As marshmallows float—oh, here comes some fun!

A raccoon in slippers collects bits of gold,
While a bear on a tricycle behaves rather bold.
They giggle as shadows jiggle and sway,
In the velvety cloak of a cheerful ballet.

Shivering Reflections

The pond winks back with a silly, sly grin,
Frogs leap out laughing, 'Where do we begin?'
Their croaks turn to giggles, a delightful affair,
As the breeze tosses leaves like they haven't a care.

A duck painted polka dots sips on some tea,
While fish tell tall tales of the ones they can't see.
And with every splash, a rumor helps bloom,
That fun finds its way, even in gloom.

Hues of Obscurity

In the corner, a monster lurks,
Just a sock with quirky quirks.
It winks and makes a silly face,
In the closet, it finds its space.

The lamp flickers, casting glee,
As shadows dance, just wait and see!
A chicken struts, a frog jumps high,
Is that a pizza slice flying by?

The Space Between Stars

Up in the sky, a star is bold,
Dressed in pajamas, feeling cold.
It trips on clouds, a clumsy sweep,
Snores so loud, it makes us weep.

The moon joins in with its old friend,
A joke so bad, they start to bend.
Comets laugh, they can't take flight,
When laughter echoes in the night.

Dappled Dreams

Beneath the tree, a nap I take,
Dreams of donuts start to bake.
A squirrel bursts in, holds a discussion,
About the latest nut nutrition.

With whispers low, the leaves confide,
Of raccoons who plan a wild ride.
Lemonade streams, giggles unfold,
Whimsical tales of acorns bold.

The Lingering Dimness

In the hallway, echoes play,
A broomstick's dance, come what may.
Whispers bubble, sounds so weird,
Even the shadows seem quite cheered!

There's a cat with a feather hat,
Doing the cha-cha, imagine that!
Each footstep sprinkles laughter bright,
In the dimness, it's party night!

Echoes in the Twilight

In the dim, we trip and sway,
With giggles that catch dusk's bouquet.
Frogs croak tunes in frothy spree,
While fireflies hold a dance decree.

A cat jumps high, lands with a thud,
While nearby dogs roll in the mud.
Mistakes are plenty, yet we all cheer,
The night is young, let's shift the gear.

We wear our hats, all skewed and wrong,
Hearing echoes of a silly song.
Raccoons join in, with eyes aglow,
Stealing snacks while we put on a show.

So here's to nights of silly fun,
Where laughter glints, and pranks are spun.
The twilight's charm, a playful tease,
In the gloom, we dance with ease.

Whispers from the Gloom

In murky halls where the giggles bloom,
We tell tall tales that chase away gloom.
The ceiling creaks; the shutters shake,
A ghost just slipped on his own cake!

With cheese and crackers for late-night bites,
We toast the moon with marshmallow flights.
A raccoon wearing a tiny hat,
Struts 'round like he's the queen of the rat!

What's that tapping? A gnome with flair?
He's cooking up trouble; we're unaware.
As whispers float in the tickling air,
Let's grab our laughs; there's joy to share!

In the depths of night, our giggles bloom,
Finding magic in the dusty room.
So bring on the joy, ignore the fears,
For whispered secrets bring laughter cheers!

Veils of Dusk

Beneath the cloak of evening's prance,
We play charades in shadowy bands.
A cat rolls by with a cheeky stare,
Its whiskers twitching like it's in a dare.

The breeze hums tunes of playful tease,
As squirrels dance high among the trees.
With silly hats and grins so wide,
We make our memories a joyride.

Wandering shapes twist and twirl,
A dance with shadows begins to swirl.
An owl hoots, "What's all the fuss?"
While we stumble and giggle with a fuss!

As night creeps in, we toast to fun,
In veils where laughter has just begun.
So join our parade in this twilight race,
For in this dusk, we find our place.

The Dance of Silhouettes

In the flicker of twilight's tender glow,
We sway like leaves in a breezy show.
A jumpy frog chronicles our plight,
As we twirl in skirts, oh what a sight!

With a wink and a wink, the shadows play,
As bustling mice lead the frolic way.
Chasing giggles and dreams so spry,
While shadows skip beneath the sky.

Tangled vines add a twist to the step,
As we cha-cha while we misstep.
Carrots parade in a wobbly row,
We dance with joy; who knew? Let's go!

In the dark, our laughter glows bright,
A merry dance, a sheer delight.
So tip your hat, take a chance,
Join us now in this silly dance.

Ghosts of Daylight

In the bright of noon, they prance and play,
Wearing hats too big, causing quite the sway.
Invisible snacks they gobble with glee,
Chasing after laughter like a bumblebee.

Their antics are silly, with quirks galore,
Jumping through puddles, knocking on the door.
They steal our sandwiches, what a surprise,
With giggles and chuckles, they just mesmerize.

In sunlight's embrace, they dance and glide,
Playing hide and seek, with nowhere to hide.
Whispers of mischief fill the warm breeze,
A parade of lightness, little trickster tease.

Though we can see them, they're hard to catch,
Just out of reach, like a runaway match.
With chubby little fingers, they wave goodbye,
Fleeting like fireflies in the evening sky.

Liminal Moments

In corners they gather, with laughter so sly,
Sipping on moonbeams and pie in the sky.
Their shenanigans peek just beneath our gaze,
Tickling our fancies in whimsical ways.

One sways on a feather, another on a shoe,
Making faces at us, as if they just knew.
With a wink and a nod, they dance along,
Singing sweet nonsense, a light-hearted song.

In the gentle stillness, they twist and twirl,
Leaving traces of giggles in a fizzy whirl.
A foot in both worlds, a wink to the night,
They pull at our dreams, just out of our sight.

Yet as we look closer, they scoff and they flee,
Whirling in circles, like a curious spree.
A moment of chaos, a fleeting delight,
These giddy occurrences tickle our light.

The Softness of Dusk

The sun takes a bow, the sky begins to blush,
As night falls softly, in a quirky hush.
Here comes the mischief, under cloaks of gray,
With goofy grins, they start their ballet.

In twilight's embrace, they tiptoe around,
Making odd shadows that dance on the ground.
Peeking from bushes, they giggle with cheer,
Elusive and silly, whispering, "Are we here?"

With their jello-like jiggles and marvelous prance,
They orchestrate mayhem, igniting a dance.
Twilight's their cover, a stage full of glee,
Where laughter erupts like waves from the sea.

As the stars twinkle on, they twirl and glide,
Casting their quirks on the incoming tide.
With winks from the moon, they gather 'round tight,
Celebrating their reign in the soft, starlit night.

The Halfway Heartbeat

In the pause of a moment, they pop like confetti,
With tongues out and laughs, their antics are ready.
They leap in the air, then land with a thud,
A giggle erupts, it's an odd little flood.

Ticklish and jumpy, like bubbles in tea,
They whirl in delight, just as spry as can be.
One plays the tuba while the other sings loud,
Creating a ruckus, oh aren't they proud?

With eyes big as saucers, they sneak and they peek,
At the shadowy light, their adrenaline's peak.
In the heart of the night, they race with a stride,
Like a silver-haired cat, with nowhere to hide.

Then with a last chuckle, they vanish from view,
Leaving behind a riddle, just for me and you.
In that awkward silence, they've gone but remain,
Stirring up laughter like a joyous refrain.

Portraits of the Half-Light

In the corners, whispers creep,
Where giggles hide and secrets leap.
A half-baked joke in every glare,
Light-hearted mischief fills the air.

With winks and grins that softly blend,
The art of laughter we intend.
Here's a giggle, there's a pun,
As day fades out, the fun's begun!

What's that lurking, don't be shy?
A rogue embrace or pie up high?
In dim-lit rooms where antics play,
A canvas brightens, come what may!

So come and see this funny sight,
A gallery of pure delight.
In half-light glow, we find our role,
A chuckling dance, a teasing stroll.

Enigmas in the Gloaming

At dusk, the riddle comes alive,
Where silly giggles strive and thrive.
Mysterious shapes with silly faces,
Twist their way through jolly places.

What's that figure taking a bow?
A silly elf or maybe a cow!
The gloaming glow, it warps the day,
Making fun, replacing gray.

Puns and jesters start to play,
In twilight's arms, the jesters sway.
Each enigma bears a grin,
In this twilight world, we all spin!

So join the fun where secrets beam,
With laughter dancing on a dream.
Embrace the odd, the jests that thrive,
In this twilight zone, we all arrive.

Silhouettes Against the Sky

Shapes pop up with big old grins,
Striking poses, let's begin!
Dancing shadows take their stand,
A comedy troupe, oh so grand!

With arms like wings and legs that flop,
Each shadow's story makes us stop.
What's that laughing by the tree?
Just a squirrel, full of glee!

As colors fade, the whispers cheer,
The silly shapes are gathered near.
Against the sky, what a sight,
These playful forms in fading light!

If you squint hard, you might just find,
A riot of fun, both wild and kind.
These silhouettes are here to say,
"Let's chuckle till the break of day!"

The Hidden Palette of Night

In the night, colors like to play,
Mixing laughter in their sway.
A brush of fun, a sprinkle of cheer,
In the dark, the giggles appear.

With twinkling stars as our light show,
The colors blend, like ice cream, whoa!
A scoop of joy, a dash of fright,
The canvas laughs with sheer delight.

Each hidden hue's a jester's song,
In the palette where we all belong.
Funny shapes and colors twist,
In the night's embrace, who could resist?

So grab your brush, paint your grin,
Join the fun and let's begin!
A hidden art, where smiles ignite,
This palette of laughter is pure delight.

The Hidden Heart of Silence

In corners dark, where giggles hide,
A mischievous mouse takes a wild ride.
Sneaking past with a crumb of cheese,
Making the cat say, "Oh please!"

Whispered secrets in the air,
The dog pretends he doesn't care.
But in the midnight's sneaky dance,
A blue jay twirls in a feathery prance.

Beneath the bed, a sock takes flight,
Chasing shadows into the night.
While the clock ticks, and the stars are bright,
Laughter echoes in a quirky delight.

So hush your voice, but not your smile,
For silence has its own goofy style.
Where every peek brings joys untold,
And the fun is never growing old.

Melodies Between Realms

A frog serenades the quiet moon,
With croaks that bring a silly tune.
Fireflies dance to the wiggly beats,
As squirrels start their midnight feasts.

In the land where giggles collide,
The clouds wear silly hats with pride.
A bumblebee leads the parade,
While the daisies sway in a grand charade.

Old ghosts laughing, just let them play,
Telling tales of a goofy day.
With every note, the world spins round,
In the realm where laughter is found.

So join the song, let your heart soar,
In the dance of joy, who could ask for more?
For in every giggle hides a thrill,
And fun is the magic that always will.

The Cradle of Uncertainty

In a land where socks simply disappear,
Unruly ducks toast with fizzy beer.
A jester juggles wobbly chairs,
While lions wear polka dot underwear.

Questions flutter like butterflies,
As giraffes recite silly lullabies.
In this cradle of whimsical thought,
Every problem's just a riddle caught.

With every stumble, a laugh is born,
And in each chaos, new dreams are worn.
For life is a game of twist and slide,
Where uncertainty is a funny guide.

So rock and roll on the edge of cheer,
Dance with the fears you hold so dear.
In the cradle where weirdness bloats,
Every doubt floats like silly boats.

A Whisper Past the Horizon

As day sinks low, a whisper hums,
About a bear who juggles plums.
A cactus sings with fervent glee,
While mountains join in harmony.

Onward floats a nonsensical kite,
Telling tales of a duck in flight.
In the distance, laughter's glow,
Bouncing on the breeze, just go with the flow!

The waves chuckle, the sand joins in,
With every giggle, dreams begin.
So let the world fade into fun,
As every jape is never done.

A phantom prance across the shore,
A silly question, just ask for more.
For in the whispers that roam so free,
Every moment's a joke, wait and see!

The Space Where Light Stops

In the corner where the brightness wanes,
A sock appears with its mysteries and stains.
It dances alone, without a care,
While the cat looks on, plotting a snare.

The dust bunnies hold a grand parade,
With choreographed moves that never fade.
They twirl and leap, gaining the floor,
In the space where light dares not explore.

The fridge hums softly, a secret song,
Reminding me that I don't belong.
It hides my leftovers and some old fries,
While I search for a snack and dodge their eyes.

The remote control, oh, what a trick!
It vanishes fast; it must be slick.
But I'm convinced it's planning a scheme,
To hide during moments I start to dream.

Phantoms in the Underbrush

In the thickets where the laughter hides,
Ghosts of garden gnomes laugh at the tides.
With their pointy hats and silly grins,
They concoct mischievous plots with spins.

The spiders weave in a sassy way,
Knitting webs for a bad hair day.
Caterpillars giggle, tucked up tight,
Thinking that's how they'll take flight at night.

Squirrels hold meetings and gather snacks,
Debating the merits of humorous hacks.
They share many tales of acorn theft,
While plotting their next great woodland quest.

The bushes rustle with a playful screech,
As beetles debate who'll be the first to breach.
A snail, full of dreams and silliness,
Takes a selfie with a dandelion, all agog.

Beyond the Day's Brightness

When the sun dips low, the moon comes out,
With a wink and a grin, there's no doubt.
Stars crack jokes from their heavenly perch,
While comets zoom by, a wild search.

The night owls hoot with a comedic flair,
Dancing on rooftops, without a care.
They're the stand-up crew of the twilight scene,
With punchlines sharp, and antics obscene.

Fireflies glow like tiny stage lights,
Encouraging laughter in the cooler nights.
Their flickering forms spark jokes on the rise,
As crickets chirp in perfect reprise.

The moon makes a face, all round and chubby,
While the breeze carries laughter, warm and snubby.
In this whimsical world, full of delight,
The night plays host to a hilarious sight.

Where Time Takes a Breather

In a hiding spot where clocks giggle,
Time takes a break, just to wiggle.
It stretches out, oh so carefree,
Playing hopscotch under the old oak tree.

A calendar flops, its pages in disarray,
As it celebrates each forgotten day.
Minutes and seconds with silly faces,
Engage in a game of hidden places.

Each tick and tock sings a funny song,
As they mess around without a plan along.
Sundials laugh, basking in warm sunlight,
While hours frolic, endlessly in flight.

In this whimsical realm where time takes rest,
Laughter echoes; it's a festive quest.
So let us join in, with smiles in hand,
For every tick is a joke that's grand.

Cerulean Dreams at Dusk

The moon wears a hat that's too big,
Stars are dancing in a giant jig.
Clouds play hide and seek with the sun,
Nature's laughter has just begun.

A squirrel with shades struts in style,
While crickets perform by the mile.
The wind tells jokes in a breezy way,
As flowers wink and start to sway.

A moth flirts with a light so bright,
Only to trip in a comical flight.
A haystack laughs, 'I'm really quite plush!'
While daisies burst out, 'We're in no rush!'

The night wears a grin, it's a festive sight,
With shadows that dance till the morning light.
In this silly place where giggles roam,
The twilight wraps us in its warm home.

Beneath the Canopied Veil

Under the leaves, where giggles play,
A raccoon wears shoes in a curious way.
The trees crack jokes with their rustling leaves,
And butterflies wear their silly sleeves.

A chipmunk juggles acorns with flair,
While frogs tap dance without a care.
The owls hold court, with a wink and a hoot,
And the breezes sing tunes from a funny flute.

The shadows stretch long, like a silly cat,
Chasing its tail with a thump and a spat.
Even the brook sings a bubbly tune,
As the stars peek out; oh, what a boon!

Beneath the greens, where the mischief hides,
Laughter and giggles are the fun rides.
As night blankets the whimsical scene,
Those silly sprites come out, all serene.

Flickering Unseen Realms

In a world where giggles float and tease,
A gopher wears glasses and reads with ease.
The fireflies play tag, glowing bright,
While the crickets cheer, 'What a fun night!'

A bamboo stick winks at a passing breeze,
And whispers, 'Let's dance, if you please!'
The stars take a plunge, just for fun,
As they dip and swirl, one by one.

Behind the curtains of velvet dark,
A hedgehog strums a ukulele spark.
The rabbits hop in rhythm, so spry,
While the moon raises a brow, oh my!

In this realm where laughter is king,
Every nook sings and the shadows swing.
With giggles and gags lining the way,
The night wears a crown of bright display.

The Dance of Obscured Light

The lanterns glitter with a mischievous twinkle,
While raccoons plan a party with a sprinkle.
Mice in tuxedos prance with glee,
In a hidden nook, under a tree.

A candle flickers as if it knows,
That shadows can dance better than pros.
The bark of trees shimmies like silk,
As the night pours laughter, smooth as milk.

With each step taken, the glow bugs sway,
While owls make wisecracks in their own way.
The evening slips on a playful shoe,
And slides through the grass, just for a view.

The secret of the night—with giggles in tow,
Nudges the stars to put on a show.
In this lively spree, all spirits take flight,
In the delightful dance of the hidden light.

Threads of Indistinct Form

In the corner, something stirs,
A sock that can't find its mate.
It tiptoes near the rubber duck,
A dance of misfit fate.

The pizza slice does slyly wink,
As if it knows a secret song.
The cat just rolls her eyes and thinks,
This party's been too long.

A chair that creaks, a table sways,
With every joke that makes us howl.
The breeze joins in, a gentle tease,
A gusty friend, our silly owl.

Laughter bubbles like a brook,
As shadows play their silly games.
We chase them round the kitchen nook,
With giggles echoing our names.

Ghosts Among the Foliage

The bushes rustle, spirits laugh,
With whispers floating in the air.
A squirrel suits up for a war dance,
While we just stop and stare.

The garden gnome, two eyes aglow,
Winks at me with cheeky grin.
He knows the secrets of the night,
And all the chaos that we're in.

As fireflies flicker in delight,
A chorus sings, absurdly loud.
The pumpkins giggle with surprise,
At all the antics they allow.

We trip on roots, unravel tales,
Of how the cat once stole the show.
In foliage thick, we find the trails,
Of ghostly fun—our laughs do grow.

The Palette of Dusk

In hues of orange, pink, and gray,
The twilight spills across the scene.
A bird in flight, a blush of play,
Turns out, it's really quite a queen.

With laughter fluttering like leaves,
The sun bids us a cheeky bye.
The moon, a joker up his sleeves,
Insists we should still try to fly.

In the canvas of the night,
The stars hang low—a dazzling show.
We paint our dreams in silly light,
As giggles spin and twirl below.

A brushstroke here, a splash of fun,
The night is ours to truly claim.
The palette blends till we are one,
And whispered jokes become our fame.

Ghostly Embrace of Twilight

As twilight wraps the world in hush,
The ghosts are ready for a game.
They sneak around, but make a fuss,
A giggle-ridden, wild acclaim.

A specter trips on clumsy feet,
"Oops!" it cries, with laughter bright.
The shadows dance to their own beat,
In this delightful, spooky night.

The owls hoot with a knowing wink,
The fireflies blurt out their glee.
As silly echoes start to sync,
Like notes of whimsical decree.

With every turn, a new surprise,
The moon is blushing, stars take chase.
We ride on giggles, laughs, and sighs,
In twilight's grand, absurd embrace.

The Passage of Lingering Silence

In the hush between the giggles,
Lurks a sneeze that twists like riddles.
Hearts race when whispers take their flight,
Who snorted? Oh, what a funny sight!

Echoes bounce like rubber balls,
Caught in corners, down the halls.
A tickle here, a snort, a cough,
We laugh until the light goes off!

Chasing after jokes we throw,
Like a cat that steals the show.
In the pause, the punchlines dwell,
Pantomime and giggle swell!

When silence wraps around us tight,
We find the giggles in the night.
Silly thoughts begin to prance,
In this quiet, we laugh and dance.

Muffled Beats of the Heart

Did you hear that thump and bump?
My shoelace gave a mighty jump!
Heartbeats drum with clumsy grace,
As I trip and make a face!

In the crowd, I start to sway,
My left foot doesn't want to play.
Laughter echoes through the park,
As I stumble on a lark!

A heartbeat echoes loud and clear,
Mixing up the fun with cheer.
With every flap of silly wings,
The rhythm of joy loudly sings!

Muffled beats can't help but dance,
In the end, they have their chance.
So let's all join this merry beat,
And make our laughter feel complete!

The Soft Footfalls of Mystery

Tiptoe through the dandelions,
Socks mismatched like reptilian lions.
A ghostly creak on wooden floors,
Who stepped there, what's behind those doors?

Each soft footfall, a funny tease,
Could it be a cat with fleas?
As I sneak and try to spy,
I trip, and oh, I start to fly!

Around the corner, off I zoom,
Launch a pillow, feel the boom!
The mystery thickens, but wait, what's there?
Just my friend with beans to share!

With laughter bright and full of cheer,
We unveil who's hiding here.
Each soft footfall leads to fun,
In our game, we always run!

Lanterns of the Dimming Sky

As the sun bids twilight a cheer,
Glow-worms light up, I draw near.
A lantern flickers, oh so bright,
Spilling giggles into the night!

Balloons drift with a silly grace,
Hiccups burst in an awkward race.
Chasing laughter 'round the trees,
We wave at stars; they giggle, please!

Each lantern holds a secret grin,
As shadows dance and twirl within.
A jester in the fading light,
Filling the heart with pure delight!

The night is young, and fun's in store,
With every giggle, we explore.
Lanterns sway, and dreams take flight,
In this fading, funny twilight!

Silken Darkness

In corners where the giggles play,
And mischief dances, night and day.
The socks that vanish, oh so sly,
Are lurking where the whispers lie.

The cat, beleaguered by the moon,
Swears he heard a funny tune.
But twirling curtains caught his eye,
And now he's chasing shadows high.

A shoe half-hidden by a chair,
Claims it's the best seat anywhere.
While lightbulbs flicker, blink, and tease,
Making shadows twist and squeeze.

Under beds, where dust bunnies roam,
The heart of chaos finds a home.
Watch out! The broom's a jester keen,
In the land where laughter's unseen.

The Realm of Soft Impressions

A tickle from the ghostly light,
A playful wink in the half of night.
Mismatched slippers march in style,
As nighttime giggles run a mile.

Leftover pizza on the floor,
Wink and smile, then explore.
The fridge is singing goofy songs,
In the realm where nothing's wrong.

Candles flicker, dance, and sway,
Making mischief in their heyday.
Once a serious little flame,
Now chuckling at its funny name.

With shadows playing hopscotch still,
They tumble down with playful thrill.
Laughter echoes off the walls,
In this kingdom where humor calls.

Embraces of the Night

The moon wears glasses, quite a sight,
As owls crack jokes, what's wrong, good night?
The stars all giggle, twinkle high,
With cosmic humor painting the sky.

A raccoon sporting a monocle neat,
Oh, what a fancy furry feat!
He digs through trash, full of grace,
With witty comments in wild chase.

Creaky doors sing out a tune,
While brooms invite the night to swoon.
With mischief wrapped in blanket folds,
The dark reveals the tales it holds.

A pair of shoes, left by the door,
Decide it's time to dance once more.
They spin and slide with pure delight,
In embraces spun from silly night.

Unseen Corners of Light

In quiet nooks the giggles swell,
A feather floats from a wishing well.
Around the lamp, the insects prance,
As shadows join this lively dance.

A toaster pops with cheeky grace,
Offering crumbs no one can trace.
While butterflies with silly hats,
Flit by the echoes of sleepy rats.

The clock, it ticks a quirky rhyme,
Every hour just feels like time.
With hands that wave, both left and right,
In unseen corners, pure delight.

The giggling curtain starts to sway,
As ghosts of laughter come to play.
What's that? A sock just made a leap,
In a world where silliness won't sleep.

Filtering Through Twilit Leaves

In the twilight where cats often play,
Squirrels joke 'bout the leaves on display.
A raccoon, with flair, wears a hat of green,
While crickets hum tunes, quite the unseen.

Under branches where giggles will roam,
Branches wear glasses, declaring them home.
A feast of the odd – nuts and some cheese,
As fireflies buzz by, dancing with ease.

Caterpillars argue who's prettiest dressed,
While beetles compete for the title of best.
They all join together, a comedy show,
As the moonlight chuckles, shining its glow.

The Veil of the Twilight Realm

In a realm where the lights flirt and tease,
A turtle finds moments of sheer expertise.
He teaches the snails how to dance in a line,
While frogs make a choir, croaking in time.

The trees wear their hats made of wisps and of dreams,
As whispers of laughter drift down in sweet beams.
A mouse with a trumpet leads high-pitched parades,
While owls sell popcorn to cast curious shades.

A dandelion's poof sends a spark in the night,
Juggling with wishes and giggles in flight.
All creatures unite in this fanciful haze,
As night gently chuckles, lost in its praise.

Stories Hidden in the Gloom

In corners of dusk where the critters conspire,
A hedgehog builds tales that the stars will admire.
With a wink and a wiggle, he spins yarns galore,
As raccoons take bets on who'll snore the loudest.

Beneath the old oak, a squirrel cracks jokes,
While fireflies giggle and string like fine folks.
They dance to the rhythm of crickets and tune,
Inventing new legends beneath the round moon.

A ghost of a rabbit tells tales of delight,
If you peek in the glade, he's a marvelous sight.
With each goofy giggle, the darkness feels bright,
And secrets turn silly in the soft, starry night.

Faded Contexts of Color

In corners where laughter has faded a bit,
Colors mix up and refuse to commit.
Blue argues with yellow, who claims it's a joke,
While gray turns to pink and simply goes broke.

A rainbow in hiding decides it's too shy,
So he colors the clouds while the sun hangs nearby.
They toss around jokes in a spectrum of smiles,
As giggles float up, carrying colorful miles.

Mismatched socks dance as if lost in the fray,
They bicker and wiggle; it's their style to play.
In a canvas where silliness mingles with glee,
Each hue spills a story, crafting bright banter spree.

Lost Among the Grays

In a world that's dim and bright,
I tripped on a ghostly kite.
It floated past, a silly tease,
Bounding off with reckless ease.

My socks are mismatched, what a sight,
I danced with socks in pure delight.
The wind laughed loud, the sky turned blue,
Who knew gray could bring such a view?

A zebra snickered, stripes in play,
He offered tea and a scone on tray.
I said, "No thanks, I'm quite content,
In this gray land, I'm heaven-sent!"

So here I stand, lost but free,
Gray skies can spark such laughter, you see.
With ghosts and gags in shifting light,
Life's a comedy, what a flight!

Tensions in the Twilight

A squirrel debated, 'Twas dinner time,
Would it be acorns or bubblegum crime?
He juggled nuts with quite the flair,
Oh, twilight's tension hung in the air.

A cat tiptoed, ready to pounce,
On shadows that danced in a rhythmic bounce.
But tripped on a leaf, what a surprise,
Fell into laughter, the sun on the rise.

Two owls were caught in a quarrel of hoots,
Over who wore the fanciest boots.
Their feathers ruffled, a sight to behold,
Twilight's tension turned funny and bold.

So as the day starts to descend,
I chuckle at all the quirks they blend.
Life's a jest in the dusky light,
Where laughter blooms, everything's bright!

Palette of the Unlit

Colors giggle as they wait,
In jars unopened, can't tempt fate.
A painter stumbles, spills bright green,
The mess becomes a scene obscene.

A brush or two joined in the fun,
Danced like fools 'neath the setting sun.
Mixing hues, they painted with glee,
An abstract work, who could disagree?

Paint cans tumbled, pots took flight,
Chasing each other into the night.
The unlit shadows laughed and spun,
Creating chaos, oh what a run!

With every stroke and every drip,
Art snickers, gives a playful quip.
In this palette of unlit dreams,
Life's a canvas, bursting at the seams!

The Call of Fading Echoes

Echoes giggled as they flew,
A call for help, or just a view?
In the twilight, they played peekaboo,
Lost in laughter, a fading crew.

Whispers floated, light as air,
"Can you catch dreams? They're quite rare!"
I reached for one, but it slipped away,
Fading echoes just want to play.

A dog barked back at the fading cheer,
Chasing echoes that danced near.
With each bark, the echoes would tease,
A slapstick show in the evening breeze.

So let them fade, let them jive,
In the realm where giggles thrive.
With every call and every jest,
Fading echoes know how to jest!

The Quietude Beneath the Surface

In the stillness, fish conspire,
To tell secrets of their choir.
Turtles grinning, a playful tease,
While bubbles dance beneath the trees.

A crab with shades, quite the sight,
Winks at a shrimp, doing it right.
The sunbeams tickle, laughter sings,
As seaweed twirls on buoyant strings.

Jellyfish giggle in pixel hues,
While starfish argue about their shoes.
Clams clap hands in a silent cheer,
Who needs a stage when water's near?

Beneath the waves, the jokes unfold,
A comic show, yet still so bold.
In the quiet, a banquet waits,
For our sea friends and their hilarious mates.

Elusive Figures in Stillness

In the park where shadows play,
Figures strut in a ballet.
A dog in shades, so suave and sly,
Chasing its tail as if to fly.

A cat with sass on a sunny ledge,
Pretends to purr, but then makes a pledge.
To conquer all that sparkles bright,
With a meow that's fit for the night.

Birds gossip over crumbs so sweet,
While squirrels plot their daring feat.
An acorn dropped, a slip, a tumble,
In laughter's grasp, they all just fumble.

The park's a stage of winks and grins,
Where laughter dances, and joy begins.
In stillness, life blooms ever so bright,
With every giggle, a pure delight.

Gradients of Forgotten Tales

On the canvas of twilight's grace,
Old stories twirl in a silly race.
A turtle in glasses reads by the shore,
While fishes gather, begging for more.

The wise old owl drops a quip,
As raccoons fail to hold their grip.
They tumble down with a furry crash,
Splitting their sides, they laugh and splash.

Colors blend in twilight's frame,
To paint the night with funny names.
The moon whispers to stars so spry,
"Why don't you tell a joke or try?"

Between the hues of tales long spun,
Laughter echoes—oh, what fun!
In gradients bright, we spin and sway,
Unraveling giggles at end of day.

The Unseen Chronicles

There's a world unseen with giggles galore,
Where kites take flight and then hit the floor.
A wind that whispers jokes to the skies,
While clouds roll by with mischievous sighs.

Lawn gnomes gossip in silent throngs,
About the neighbor's not-so-funny songs.
With hats tipped low and grins so wide,
They chuckle quietly, trying to hide.

In the tangle of vines, a raccoon sneaks,
Dressed in a cape, it peeks and squeaks.
While fireflies flash, a dance of delight,
Illuminating giggles lost from sight.

The unseen tales of a whimsical night,
Bring laughter forth and pure delight.
In each corner, a joke takes flight,
As the world of wonders spins into light.

Subtle Traces of the Unseen

A sneaky rustle in the night,
Cats blame the ghosts for their fright.
Socks disappear, it's quite a game,
As if they vanished, never the same.

A wink from the moon, with a chuckle so sly,
Creatures giggle, as they pass by.
Coffee cups clink in a playful toast,
To all the things that tease and boast.

Lurking beneath the couch's wide grin,
Mismatched shoes chuckle, where to begin?
The fridge hums tunes of a dance so grand,
While crumbs form parties — oh, isn't it grand?

With echoes of laughter, a lighthearted spree,
A tickle from breezes, as wild as can be.
What mischief awaits in the silence so deep?
Join the fun, but don't forget your leap!

Mysteries in the Dim

Under the bed, what a sight,
Sock puppets waltz in the mellow light.
A broomstick whispers, secrets unclear,
As dust bunnies giggle, without any fear.

The shadows muster a party soirée,
With giggles and wiggles, in their own way.
A lopsided grin from a lamp nearby,
Gives a wink, "Don't be shy!"

The cat looks baffled, hair standing tall,
Chasing the laughter? A funny recall.
Candles flicker, igniting the fun,
With mysteries blooming, one by one.

In every nook, hilarity brews,
With whispers and rustles, sharing the news.
So take a step back, let your laughter roll,
In the world's funny twists, let joy take its toll.

When Darkness Comes to Play

In the twilight dim, pranks start to swell,
Jam jars giggle, when they hear a bell.
A sneaky raccoon with a mask so sly,
Makes off with leftovers, oh me, oh my!

A flicker of light, and off they all fly,
Giggling so hard, it's quite the spy.
The vacuum cleaner plays peek-a-boo,
While slippers assume they can walk and chew.

The pantry whispers, a secret so sweet,
It's midnight snack time, a delicious treat.
Creatures of comfort, in corners they hide,
Wait for the laughter, and bounce with pride.

In this kooky hour, where all things bend,
Let silliness rule, let the giggles extend.
For when the night plays, no worries remain,
Join the mischief, and lose all restraint!

Lurkers in the Periphery

With every corner, there's a giggle or two,
A squirrel's got plans, who knew he could chew?
Plant pots whisper, 'Did you hear that?'
While shadows revel, where the mishaps sat.

Fleeting glances of something absurd,
As cookie jars conspire, it's also inferred.
The tin cans dance, their music so bright,
In the kitchen, chaos follows delight.

Lampshades chuckle, as they throw their light,
Creating odd shapes that dance through the night.
A hush, then a shudder, a curious sight,
As the broom joins the fun, ready to fight.

Endless laughter creeps through the air,
Each nook and cranny wishes to share.
So come join the jesters in this brave play,
And laugh with the rhymes till the break of day!

Echoes in Twilight

In the dim light, I trip on a cat,
My slippers slide, I look like a brat.
The clock strikes nine, it's time for a snack,
But first, my socks have gone on the attack.

There's laughter brewing under the moon,
A chorus of crickets joins in, their tune.
The blender whirs like a rickety bike,
I call it 'dinner,' yet it's not what I like.

A dance with the shadows, a shuffle of feet,
I wave hello to my ghostly retreat.
They giggle and tease, what a silly affair,
As I trip over shoes that just won't be where.

And when the lamp flickers, I jump with a shout,
Is it just the cats, or something to doubt?
In echoes of twilight, we sway and we play,
Who knew this old house would have such a sway?

Where Light Fades

In corners where dimness begins to conspire,
I found a lost sock, haunted by fire.
The dog gave a bark, but it sounded like chat,
As if it was saying, 'Don't dare sit, what a brat!'

The chairs told me stories from long, weary days,
Of grand feasts and shenanigans, wild, funny ways.
They creaked and they groaned like an old man's back,
Saying, 'We've seen it all, but please hold the snack!'

A shadow once whispered, 'You've stepped in the goo',
It seemed just as natural, but alas, it was true.
With each silly stumble, I laughed 'til I cried,
In the twilight of laughter, my worries all fried.

A dance with the shadows, the cat played along,
We tangoed through chaos, to our own silly song.
In the space where the light fades, we cherish the fun,
Where moments turn giggles until we are done.

The Quiet Murmur of Gloom

In the still of the night, where echoes reside,
I lost my left shoe, now this isn't that wide.
The fridge starts to hum a lullaby tune,
While I search for snacks like a raccoon in June.

The curtain flutters, it's planning a dance,
While I trip on a plant, what a clownish chance.
'You've watered me well,' it seems to bestow,
While I scratch my head, where did the sock go?

The shadows conspire, they gather quite near,
With whispers of mischief, I know they can hear.
But laughter erupts, drowning out all the gloom,
As I waltz with the chaos right here in my room.

So let's raise a toast to the fun in despair,
To the silly old phantoms that hang in midair.
We'll murmur and cackle, a toast to the night,
Where the quiet finds joy, and shadows take flight.

Hues of Dappled Silence

In colors of quiet where nonsense resides,
I painted my walls with purple and glides.
The dog wore a hat, it's a sight just to see,
He's plotting with squirrels, oh dear, where is me?

Under dappled leaves where stories conjoin,
I lost track of time, and the weird paths I join.
My dreams creep around like a cat in a tree,
Whisking up nonsense while eating your pea.

The silence chuckles, it tickles my toes,
As I mimic a dancer with nobody knows.
A moonbeam strikes odd; I slip on a chore,
And tumble headlong, bumping into the door.

Yet with each clumsy fall, I laugh and I sway,
For the hues of my silence ignite silly play.
In the quirky, the weird, the laughter shall bask,
In the dappled light's secrets, I leave you to ask.

Murmurs Beneath the Canopy

Beneath the trees where whispers play,
Squirrels debate on the best acorn way.
Chirping crickets share their news,
While curious raccoons steal the shoes.

A breeze tickles leaves in a silly dance,
As chipmunks giggle at nature's chance.
Frogs in the pond hold a croaky jest,
While owls just roll their eyes at the rest.

Sunlight filters through like a jester's cheer,
Making shadows wiggle, spreading good beer.
Every rustle and flutter, a comical plot,
In this hidden grove, joy's never forgot.

Laughter erupts from each leafy nook,
Every critter's giggle, a quirky hook.
In this canopy's laughter, life plays its role,
Creating a riddle for the cautious soul.

Shadows in the Haze

In a fog where peculiars waddle about,
A rabbit debates with a sprouting sprout.
A duck in sunglasses quacks with flair,
While a hedgehog giggles without any care.

Crickets hold court in a hazy scene,
Joking that grass is the new cuisine.
As the sun peeks in, they scurry and flee,
Like an old couple trying to find their tea.

The haze hugs the ground with a cheeky grin,
Where shadows throw fits, trying to spin.
"Can we dance?" asks a snail, feeling bold,
But his slow little wiggle's too cute to scold.

In this misty circus where laughter expands,
Everyone dances, forgetting their plans.
Just a frolic of humor, where all's just a game,
In the dim little corners, we all stay the same.

Half-Light Reveries

As twilight descends in a dreamy spree,
Fireflies gather for an evening tea.
Frogs in tuxedos croak in delight,
Planning a ball for the silliest night.

Murky figures twist in playful distress,
A raccoon spills snacks, creating a mess.
Laughter erupts as they chase the moon,
In this whimsical world, mischief's a tune.

The half-light winks with a mischievous gleam,
Mice in top hats take over the dream.
Each flutter and giggle a delightful surprise,
As they plot their mischief beneath the skies.

In this twilight riddle, the humor's alive,
Where the quirkiest creatures happily thrive.
With a wink and a nod, they whisper and play,
Creating a joy that won't fade away.

Secrets in the Twilight

As dusk wraps the day in a silvery coat,
A hedgehog strums tunes on a floating boat.
The wind whispers jokes to the leaves on the ground,
While crickets jump in for a giggling round.

A raccoon sneaks snacks from the picnic spread,
While fireflies twinkle, lighting their tread.
"Is it a party?" a chubby bear grins,
With a belly that jiggles, inviting all sins.

In this twilight, whispers swirl with glee,
As owls crack wise with their eyes full of tea.
Squirrels toss acorns like confetti galore,
Celebrating life with a cheeky encore.

In this secretive hour where laughter gleams bright,
Every corner's filled with a playful delight.
So come join the frolic, let your worries slide,
In the twilight's embrace, where the gigglers abide.

Spheres of the Unshown

In a room full of socks, they plot and conspire,
To escape from the drawer, their ultimate desire.
They laugh at the humans, so clueless and lost,
As they plan their great heist, no matter the cost.

A cat leaps around, and they all hold their breath,
In a dance of pure chaos, they flirt with their death.
They tumble and roll, a soft fabric swirl,
In a game of tag, their cotton flags unfurl.

When the sun starts to drop, their giggles take flight,
In the beam of the moon, all the socks stay up bright.
They pull little pranks, under cover of night,
As humans snooze softly, they frolic in delight.

So if you find socks, in mismatched array,
Remember their party that took place today.
They may seem quite tame, but it's all just a show,
In the spheres of the unshown, their antics still glow.

The Companion of Dusk

There's a guy named Fred, who talks to his chair,
Claiming it listens, while we stand and stare.
At dusk he recites tales of dragons and knights,
To a piece of old furniture, under soft light.

He brings it a snack, a cookie or two,
And whispers sweet nothings, like it's a guru.
The neighbors just grin, as they peek through the blinds,
To see Fred and his buddy, with very good finds.

As twilight descends, they plot world domination,
With plans that revolve around cookie creation.
They laugh at the moon, as they quietly scheme,
A friendship forever, it seems like a dream.

So if you hear giggles at the end of your street,
Know that Fred and his chair have planned something sweet.
With cookies and laughter, they'll conquer the night,
In the company of dusk, everything feels right.

Weavings of the Unspoken

In the attic they gather, those dust bunnies bold,
Spinning yarns of their travels, both daring and old.
With each little leap, they'll tell their grand tale,
Of kingdoms afar and a dangerous snail.

They knit woolen socks, for the toes of the day,
With polka dots, stripes, making quite the display.
Each stitch is a giggle, each knot is a tease,
As they dream of adventures among the tall trees.

While humans are busy, these creatures take flight,
In a world of bright colors, they sparkle with light.
They party till morning, at a rate quite absurd,
In weavings of secrets, their laughter is heard.

So if you find fluff in unusual places,
It's just the bunnies, sharing their paces.
With blankets of joy, they cover the night,
In their whimsical realm, everything feels right.

Threads in the Embrace of Night

There's a textile affair, with threads all around,
In the embrace of night, a stitching rebound.
The buttons have secrets, the zippers hold dreams,
As they twirl and they leap under moonlight beams.

With laughter they gather, in patterns galore,
Unraveling tales from the closet's great core.
The ribbons tell stories of dances and flings,
While the pockets just giggle at all of these things.

As midnight draws near, they plan a grand ball,
With sequins and glitter, they'll dazzle them all.
The socks and the shirts will take on a new role,
In threads of the night, each garment a soul.

So if you hear rustling, don't think it's a fright,
It's just fabric friends, enjoying the night.
In their joyous parade, they sing and they play,
In the threads of the embrace, they dance till the day.

Harmony of the Undergrowth

In the twinkling glen, critters conspire,
To dance with the ferns and play in the fire.
A squirrel with a hat, oh what a sight,
Is he off to a party, or just feeling bright?

The ants toss a party, with crumbs galore,
While worms do the twist, begging for more.
A frog serenades, his voice quite absurd,
As a snail breaks the beat, it's totally blurred.

The mushrooms are bobbing, as if they can groove,
While the grasshoppers jump, trying to prove.
It's just another day, in the underbrush,
With laughter and giggles, never a rush.

Colors of the Unrevealed

In the garden of secrets, colors collide,
A rainbow of veggies, all trying to hide.
Beets wear a wig, like they're off to a show,
While carrots gossip, putting on quite a glow.

Tomatoes are blushing, they just can't believe,
They've sprouted a rumor, no way to retrieve.
The radishes chuckle, beneath leafy trees,
As they roll in the dirt, like they're aiming to tease.

Beneath the green cabbages, tales start to unfurl,
In a world of the whacky, it's truly a whirl.
With every big bloom, a new story is spun,
This garden of laughter, oh what fun it's begun!

The Gentle Clutch of Night

As twilight creeps in, the critters convene,
In whispers and giggles, the funniest scene.
Fireflies flicker, like stars in disguise,
While bats play tag under moonlit skies.

The owls make jokes, with their serious looks,
While raccoons raid picnics with squeaks and with crooks.

A fox tells a tale, wrapped up in delight,
Of when he stole cookies, under the night.

The gentle embrace of the cool evening air,
Leaves room for the laughter, free from all care.
With laughter so rich, the night stretches on,
As all the night critters bask 'til the dawn.

Enfolded in Softness

In the softness of dusk, where mischief convenes,
Bunnies don slippers, in velvety jeans.
They hop through the fields, with a skip in their stride,
Sharing tales of the carrots they sneakily hide.

Kittens roll over, in a plush, fuzzy heap,
While puppies chase moonbeams, in playful leaps.
Under star-lit blankets, they snuggle so tight,
In a fluffball of joy, as they giggle in delight.

The night wraps around them, like a warm hug so dear,
Bringing fun, fluffy dreams, replacing all fear.
With giggles and purrs, the world seems just right,
In this cozy embrace of the gentle night.